D0116748

★ ★

NEW MEXICO

by Linda S. Weiss-Malik

GARETH**STEVENS**

A Member of the WRC Media Family of Companies

Please visit our web site at: www.garethstevens.com
For a free color catalog describing Gareth Stevens Publishing's
list of high-quality books, call 1-800-542-2595 (USA) or
1-800-387-3178 (Canada).

Library of Congress Cataloging-in-Publication Data

Weiss-Malik, Linda S.
  New Mexico / Linda S. Weiss-Malik.
    p. cm. — (Portraits of the states)
  Includes bibliographical references and index.
  ISBN-10: 0-8368-4705-9 — ISBN-13: 978-0-8368-4705-5 (lib. bdg.)
  ISBN-10: 0-8368-4722-9 — ISBN-13: 978-0-8368-4722-2 (softcover)
  1. New Mexico—Juvenile literature. I. Title. II. Series.
  F796.3.W45   2007
  978.9—dc22   2006004073

This edition first published in 2007 by
Gareth Stevens Publishing
A Weekly Reader® Company
1 Reader's Digest Road
Pleasantville, NY 10570-7000 USA

This edition copyright © 2007 by Gareth Stevens, Inc.

Editorial direction: Mark J. Sachner
Project manager: Jonatha A. Brown
Editor: Catherine Gardner
Art direction and design: Tammy West
Picture research: Diane Laska-Swanke
Indexer: Walter Kronenberg
Production: Jessica Morris and Robert Kraus

Picture credits: Cover, pp. 4, 18 © Tom Bean; p. 5 © Art Today; pp. 6, 20
© Nancy Carter/North Wind Picture Archives; pp. 8, 9, 10 © North Wind
Picture Archives; p. 12 © CORBIS; pp. 15, 16, 22, 24, 25, 28 © John Elk III;
p. 26 © James P. Rowan; p. 27 © Jeff Greenberg/PhotoEdit; p. 29 © Marc
Muench/CORBIS

Printed in the United States of America

2 3 4 5 6 7 8 9 11 10 09 08 07

CONTENTS

Words that are defined in the Glossary appear
in **bold** the first time they are used in the text.

On the Cover: The Native Americans of New Mexico have long lived in
flat-roofed homes like these. This type of building is common here.

CHAPTER

★ ★ ★ ★ ★ ★ ★ ★

1

Introduction

What comes to mind when you think of New Mexico? Native people who built homes that reached five stories high? Explorers looking for treasure? Outlaws from the days of the Wild West? Or ships from outerspace? In New Mexico, the people have exciting tales to tell.

This state is also known for its great natural beauty. New Mexico has rugged mountains, grassy plains, and colorful deserts. Most days bring sunshine, blue skies, and flaming sunrises and sunsets. It is no wonder New Mexico is called the Land of Enchantment!

So, come for a visit. Listen to the tales and explore the state's beauty. Share the excitement of New Mexico!

Shiprock is a rocky peak in the northwestern corner of the state. It is a holy place for the Navajo.

The state flag of New Mexico.

NEW MEXICO FACTS

- Became the 47th U.S. State: January 6, 1912
- Population (2005): 1,928,384
- Capital: Santa Fe
- Biggest Cities: Albuquerque, Las Cruces, Santa Fe, Rio Rancho
- Size: 121,356 square miles (314,311 square kilometers)
- Nickname: The Land of Enchantment
- State Tree: Piñon
- State Flower: Yucca
- State Mammal: Black bear
- State Bird: Roadrunner

History

Native Americans have lived in New Mexico for more than ten thousand years. By the 1500s, many tribes lived there. The Navajos, Apaches, and Acomas were among them. They hunted animals for their meat and skins. They grew corn, beans, and squash. Some tribes herded sheep, too.

Early Europeans

Marcos de Niza came here from Mexico in 1539. He was a Spanish priest who hoped to teach the Natives about his religion. His trip did not go well. The Natives killed one of his men, and Niza left. He told other people he had seen a land full of treasure, so more explorers set out to find it. They reached New Mexico, but they did not find gold and jewels there.

In 1598, Don Juan de Oñate claimed this area for Spain. He and his men built the town of San Gabriel. It was the

Today, you can see the ruins of Native villages at Chaco Culture National Historic Park.

first European settlement in New Mexico. Oñate and his men also fought the Acomas. They killed many of them. They took others captive and made them slaves.

In 1610, Santa Fe became the capital of the Spanish **colony**. More Spaniards came. Most of them were priests. In 1680, the Natives **rebelled** against the priests and forced the Spanish out. But they did not hold the land for long. By 1694, the Spanish had taken the land back. They held this area for more than one hundred twenty-five years.

Three Groups of Settlers

In the 1700s, many settlers came to this area from Spain and Mexico. They founded towns such as Albuquerque. Thirty thousand people lived in the colony by 1800. A few years later, people from the United States began to arrive. The first newcomers were trappers. Before long, farmers and traders moved here, too.

In 1821, Mexico broke away from the country of Spain. Mexico took over the land in New Mexico.

By this time, three groups of people lived in this area. One group was the Native Americans. The second group was the Hispanics.

During the 1800s, thousands of settlers came to Santa Fe in covered wagons.

FUN FACTS

What's in a Name?

New Mexico was named by the early Spanish explorers. They named it after Mexico, the place they had come from. They called the land they explored *Nuevo Mexico*. In Spanish, these words mean "New Mexico."

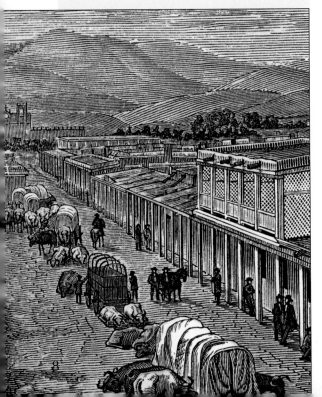

They are people who can trace their families back to Mexico, Spain, and other places where Spanish is spoken. The third group was the Anglos. They are white people who speak English. Many Anglos thought they were better than the Hispanics and the Native people.

A New Territory

In 1846, the United States and Mexico went to war.

8

Two hundred years ago, the Native people of New Mexico lived in simple homes.

They fought to get control over land in what is now the southwestern United States. The U.S. Army took over Santa Fe during the war. After two years, the United States won the war and took over most of New Mexico.

In 1850, the New Mexico **Territory** was set up. Later, the United States bought more land from Mexico and added it to the New Mexico territory. Many more settlers moved here. Some of these settlers came to raise cattle and crops. Some of them came to sell goods and mine for gold. And some came seeking adventure.

The Wild West

In the late 1800s, ranchers, farmers, shopkeepers, and miners sometimes fought. They fought over land and the right to do business in New Mexico. Many men carried guns at this time, and some were quick to use them. New Mexico was a dangerous place. It was part of the Wild West.

The U.S. government wanted more land for the

Anglos. It tried to force the Natives in New Mexico to move to **reservations**. Many Navajos and Apaches did not want to leave their homes. They fought with the Army off and on for many years. In 1886, they finally gave up. Then, all of the Natives in the territory had to live on reservations.

The 1900s

In time, the government brought law and order to the land. Then, in 1912, New Mexico became a U.S. state.

The state had a large Hispanic **population**. Hispanics owned many businesses here. They also served in the armed forces and fought in

IN NEW MEXICO'S HISTORY

Native Soldiers

Native Americans have served in the U.S. armed forces since the late 1800s. They have fought in many wars. During World War II, Navajo soldiers made up a code based on their own language. Then, these "code talkers" sent secret messages for the U.S. Marines. The enemy never cracked their code. At that time, these loyal Native Americans did not have the right to vote in state elections in New Mexico. The state finally gave them that right in 1948.

By 1900, Native families like this one were living on reservations.

Famous People of New Mexico

Robert Goddard

Born: October 5, 1882, Worcester, Massachusetts

Died: August 10,1945, Baltimore, Maryland

Robert Goddard is known as the "father of modern rocketry." He worked in Roswell in the 1930s. There, he built rockets that used liquid fuel. No one had done this before. Goddard became the first man to build a liquid-fueled rocket that flew faster than the speed of sound. One of his rockets flew 9,000 feet (2,743 meters) high. Goddard led the way in creating powerful, high-flying rockets.

wars. They worked in the government, too. In 1916, the people of New Mexico elected the first Hispanic governor in U.S. history. Twelve years later, they sent the first Hispanic American to the U.S. Senate. Even so, many Hispanics in New Mexico were poor.

In the 1930s, prices for goods and crops fell across the country. People lost their jobs, and businesses closed. This was the Great Depression. The people of New Mexico suffered. The U.S. government started projects that put people back to work. Workers in New Mexico built dams on some of the state's rivers. Lakes formed behind the dams and provided water for farms.

The nation entered World War II in 1941. During the

One of the first atomic bombs explodes near Alamogordo.

war, the U.S. government built Los Alamos. It brought top scientists to live in this town. These people created the first atomic bomb. This helped the United States and its **allies** win the war.

New Mexico Today

After the war ended, more people moved to this state. Some people came to work for the government. Others came to enjoy New Mexico's beauty and to create art and crafts. Today, the state is still growing.

Some people worry that New Mexico will run short of water one day. The state's leaders are working to make sure that the state will have enough water for all.

IN NEW MEXICO'S HISTORY

Wildfire!

The biggest **wildfire** in New Mexico's history took place in May 2000. It started when fire marshals lit a small fire to clear some dead brush. Soon, the fire blazed out of control. Over the next few weeks, it burned more than 47,000 acres (19,020 hectares). The fire burned hundreds of homes and other buildings in Los Alamos.

★ ★ ★ Time Line ★ ★ ★

1539	Marcos de Niza is the first European to visit New Mexico.
1680	Native Americans rebel against the Spanish. Fourteen years later the Spanish take control again.
1821	Mexico wins its freedom from Spain and claims New Mexico.
1822	The Santa Fe Trail opens.
1848	The United States wins the Mexican War. New Mexico now belongs to the United States.
1878–1881	Farmers, ranchers, and shopkeepers fight for control of the land in New Mexico.
1912	New Mexico becomes the forty-seventh U.S. state.
1930	Robert Goddard moves to New Mexico, where he tests the first rockets to break the sound barrier.
1945	The first atomic bomb is created at Los Alamos.
1948	Native Americans in New Mexico gain the right to vote.
1994	Sid Gutierrez becomes the first Hispanic to lead a space shuttle mission.
2000	The biggest wildfire in New Mexico's history destroys property in and around Los Alamos.

People

Fewer than two million people live in New Mexico. Yet the state is growing fast. Since 1990, its population has grown by 25 percent.

Most New Mexicans live in cities. More than one-third of all the people in the state live in or near Albuquerque. It is the largest city in New Mexico. It is also one of the fastest growing cities in the nation. Las Cruces and Santa Fe are the next largest cities. Santa Fe is also the oldest capital city in the United States. It

Hispanics
This chart shows the different racial backgrounds of people in New Mexico. In the 2000 U.S. Census, 42.1 percent of the people in New Mexico called themselves Latino or Hispanic. Most of them or their relatives came from places where Spanish is spoken. Hispanics do not appear on this chart because they may come from any racial background.

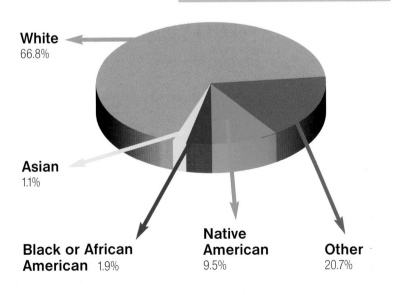

The People of New Mexico

Total Population 1,903,289

White 66.8%

Asian 1.1%

Black or African American 1.9%

Native American 9.5%

Other 20.7%

Percentages are based on the 2000 Census.

has many winding streets and old **adobe** buildings.

Three main groups of people live in New Mexico. They are Hispanics, Anglos, and Native Americans.

Hispanics and Anglos

About 42 percent of the people here are Hispanic. There is a higher percentage of Hispanics in New Mexico than in any other U.S. state. In some parts of the state, more than one-half of the people are Hispanic. Most of them or their relatives came from Mexico. Other Hispanic families have roots in Spain or in Central or South America.

The Hispanics in this state are powerful. Many of them own businesses. Some have jobs in the government. They have more power than most Hispanic groups in this country. Many of the people who have come from Mexico recently are not as well off. Some cannot speak English. They do not have a good education. They struggle to feed their families.

15

Many Native American children learn the old ways of their tribes. These children are performing the corn dance.

About 45 percent of the people in New Mexico are Anglos. They can trace their roots back to Britain, France, Germany, and other parts of Europe.

Native Americans

About one person in ten in this state is a Native. Most Natives live on reservations. The Navajos have the biggest reservation in the United States. Part of their land is in New Mexico. The Apache people have two reservations in this state. Other Native people have reservations here, too. Some Natives do not live on reservations. Most of these people live in or near New Mexico's towns and cities.

Religion

Most of the people living in New Mexico are Christians. Of these Christians, the largest group is Catholic. Most of the Hispanics in the state are Catholic. Many Baptists and Methodists live here, too.

Some of the people in the state follow Native religions. They believe in gods that were worshipped by Native tribes long ago. Some of the people mix Native ideas with Catholic beliefs.

Education

The first schools in New Mexico were run by Catholic priests. Only the rich could afford to send their children to school. The state's first free public schools were set up in 1891.

The state has three big universities. The largest

is the University of New Mexico in Albuquerque. More than one-half of all adults over age twenty-five have gone to college.

Famous People of New Mexico

Sid Gutierrez

Born: June 27, 1951, Albuquerque, New Mexico

Sid Gutierrez grew up in Albuquerque. When he was a boy, he wanted to become an astronaut. Years later, he joined the Air Force and became an outstanding pilot. In 1991, he served as a pilot on a space shuttle mission. Three years later, he was named commander of the space shuttle *Endeavour*. His flight on the *Endeavour* made history. On this flight, Gutierrez became the first Hispanic ever to lead a space shuttle mission.

The Land

New Mexico is in a part of the country called the American Southwest. It is the fifth-largest state in the country. The state is made up of three natural areas. They are the Great Plains, the mountains, and the High **Plateau**.

The Great Plains

The Great Plains lie in the eastern one-third of the state. The plains are mostly flat. Two big rivers flow through the plains. They are the Pecos River and the Canadian River.

The climate is mostly dry and sunny. Temperatures are mild. Much of the land here is covered with grasses and cactus. One type of grass, blue grama grass, is the state

The Pecos River winds its way through the eastern part of the state.

NEW MEXICO

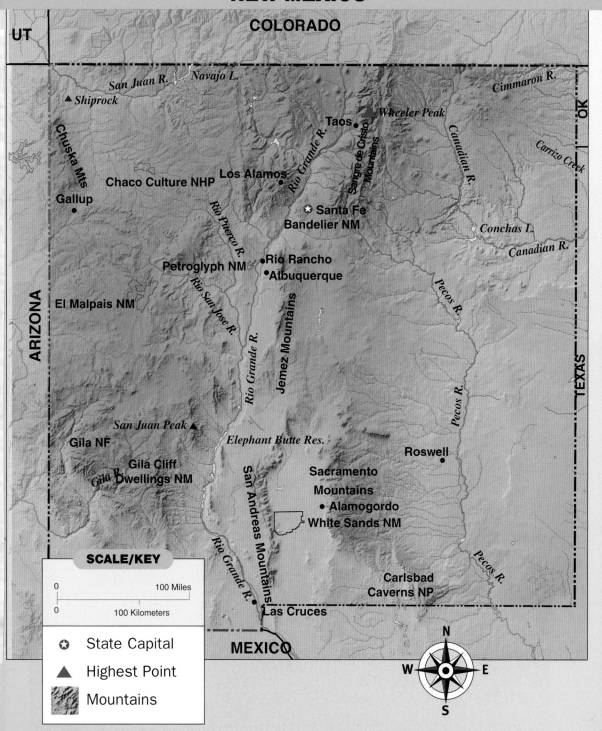

COLORADO

UT

ARIZONA

OK

TEXAS

MEXICO

San Juan R.

Navajo L.

Cimmaron R.

▲ Shiprock

Wheeler Peak

Carrizo Creek

Chuska Mts

Taos ●

Sangre de Cristo Mountains

Canadian R.

Chaco Culture NHP

Los Alamos

Rio Grande R.

Gallup ●

☆ Santa Fe
Bandelier NM

Conchas L.

Rio Puerco R.

Canadian R.

Petroglyph NM

● Rio Rancho
● Albuquerque

Pecos R.

El Malpais NM

Rio San Jose R.

Jemez Mountains

Rio Grande R.

Pecos R.

San Juan Peak ▲

Elephant Butte Res.

Gila NF

Roswell ●

Gila Cliff
Dwellings NM

Gila R.

San Andreas Mountains

Sacramento
Mountains

● Alamogordo

White Sands NM

Rio Grande R.

Carlsbad
Caverns NP

Pecos R.

Las Cruces

SCALE/KEY

0   100 Miles

0   100 Kilometers

☆ State Capital

▲ Highest Point

▦ Mountains

N
W   E
S

grass. Animals in this part of the state include coyotes, pronghorns, and prairie dogs.

The Mountains

Mountains run down the center of the state. In the north, the Rocky Mountains stand tall. To the east is the Sangre de Cristo Range. The highest point in the state is found in this range. This point is Wheeler Peak. It is 13,161 feet (4,011 m) high. Other mountains lie farther south and west. The Jemez and San Juan Ranges are two

Major Rivers
Rio Grande
1,885 miles (3,033 km)
Pecos River
500 miles (805 km)
Canadian River
906 miles (1,458 km)

of these other mountain ranges in New Mexico.

The high mountains are colder than the rest of the land in the state. Snow falls on the peaks in the winter.

The state's longest river runs through the mountains. This river is the Rio Grande.

This valley lies at the bottom of the Sangre de Cristo Mountains.

The land along this river is good for farming.

One-fourth of the state is covered with forests. Most of these forests are found on the mountains. Firs and ponderosa pines grow here. Hardwood trees include oak, maple, and birch. Animals such as mule deer, bighorn sheep, and elk live in this part of the state. Bears and bobcats can be found, too.

The High Plateau

The High Plateau covers the western part of New Mexico. It includes wide valleys and plains. Rivers have carved deep canyons in this land. In many parts of the plateau, flat-topped **mesas** rise up from the land below.

This is the driest area in the state. Deserts cover the land in the southwest. The plants of the desert include cactuses and shrubs with

FUN FACTS

A Famous Bear

In 1950, a fire swept through the Lincoln National Forest. While battling this blaze, firefighters found a bear in a tree. They rescued him and took him to a zoo. At first, the bear was called Hot Foot Teddy. Later, he became known as Smokey Bear. Smokey Bear became famous across the country as a symbol of fire safety.

small leaves. Kangaroo rats, prairie dogs, and mice are at home there. Horned lizards and snakes live in the cracks between the rocks. Farther north is the Gila National Forest. Ponderosa pines, piñons, and other trees are common. The piñon pine is the state tree. Big animals such as black bears and elk live there. Hawks and bald eagles make nests there, too.

Economy

New Mexico is home to more than fifteen thousand farms and ranches. The biggest product by far is cattle. They are raised for meat and milk. Sheep are raised here, too. Farmers grow onions, hay, and other crops. The state is also known for its spicy chili peppers.

This is one of the top mining states in the country. Oil, natural gas, copper, and coal are mined here. The state produces more **potash** than any other state.

Manufacturing and Research

Many people work in factories. Some of these workers make parts for computers. Others make cheese, meat products, and cereals. Some make gasoline and other

Copper mining is big business in New Mexico. The state ranks third in copper production.

products from oil. The state's largest oil **refinery** belongs to the Navajo nation.

The cities of Albuquerque and Los Alamos are research centers. The workers there develop high-tech weapons. The state is also home to many military bases.

Services

More people in New Mexico work in services than in any other kind of job. Service workers help other people. They work in hospitals, schools, repair shops, and other useful places.

Tourism provides many service jobs in this state. Millions of tourists come to New Mexico each year. They stay in hotels and eat in restaurants. They visit museums, parks, and ski slopes. All of these places need workers.

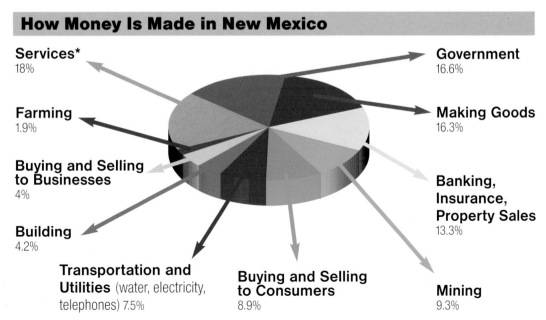

How Money Is Made in New Mexico

Services* 18%

Farming 1.9%

Buying and Selling to Businesses 4%

Building 4.2%

Transportation and Utilities (water, electricity, telephones) 7.5%

Buying and Selling to Consumers 8.9%

Government 16.6%

Making Goods 16.3%

Banking, Insurance, Property Sales 13.3%

Mining 9.3%

* Services include jobs in hotels, restaurants, auto repair, medicine, teaching, and entertainment.

Government

Santa Fe is the capital of New Mexico. It is the oldest capital city in the United States. The state's leaders work there. New Mexico's state government has three parts. They are the executive, legislative, and judicial branches.

Executive Branch

The executive branch carries out the state's laws. The governor is the leader of this branch. A team of people called the cabinet works with the governor.

New Mexico is the only state in the nation that has a round capitol building.

The Palace of the Governors was built by the Spanish in 1610. It later served as the capitol of the New Mexico Territory. Now it is a museum.

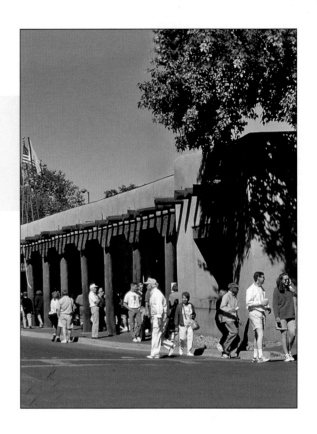

Legislative Branch

The New Mexico legislature has two parts. They are the House of Representatives and the Senate. These two groups work together to make laws for the state.

Judicial Branch

Judges and courts make up the judicial branch. Judges and courts may decide whether people who have been accused of committing crimes are guilty.

Local Government

New Mexico has thirty-three counties. Each county is run by a team of people known as commissioners. Most cities are run by a small group of people, too.

NEW MEXICO'S STATE GOVERNMENT

Executive		Legislative		Judicial	
Office	**Length of Term**	**Body**	**Length of Term**	**Court**	**Length of Term**
Governor	4 years	Senate (42 members)	4 years	Supreme (5 justices)	8 years
Lieutenant Governor	4 years	House of Representatives (70 members)	2 years	Appeals (10 judges)	8 years

CHAPTER

★ ★ ★ ★ ★ ★ ★

7

Things to See and Do

FUN FACTS

Aliens?

Roswell is the center of a very strange story. The story says that an **alien** space ship crashed near Roswell in 1947. Some people say the body of a dead alien was found after the crash! Now, Roswell is famous. Each year on July 4, thousands of people attend a **UFO** Festival in Roswell. This is a big gathering for people who believe that aliens visit the Earth.

New Mexico is a beautiful state! In the mountains, you can go hiking and enjoy great views. At White Sands National Monument, you can take peaceful walks. In Chama Valley, you can ride on a train and roll past green valleys and rugged mountains. This state has many interesting and fun things to see and do.

Outdoor and Indoor Fun

One interesting park to see is Carlsbad Caverns National Park. It is in southern New Mexico. It

Visitors admire the bright white dunes at White Sands National Monument.

is one of the world's largest cave systems. Visitors can explore some of the caves in this park.

Several national parks and monuments in New Mexico feature old **ruins**. They are great places to see how the Native people in this area once lived. One of the best parks in the state is Chaco Culture National Historical Park. It has the ruins of old pueblos. You can see more ruins at Gila Cliff Dwellings National Monument.

Each year in August, the city of Gallup hosts a huge powwow. Visitors can watch real Native **ceremonies** and dances, try Native foods, and go to a rodeo.

Famous People of New Mexico

Nancy Lopez

Born: January 6, 1957, Torrance, California

Nancy Lopez is a well-known golfer. Her family moved to Roswell when she was young. She began playing golf when she was eight years old. While she was in college, she became a **professional** golfer. During the 1970s, Lopez was named "Golfer of the Decade" by *Golf Magazine*. She won more than forty major golf matches. She is known as one of the first Hispanic female sports stars.

Hispanics make up more than 40 percent of New Mexico's population. These teenagers are performing at the state fair in Albuquerque.

Famous People of New Mexico

Billy the Kid

Born: November 23, 1859, New York, New York
Died: July 13, 1881, Fort Sumner, New Mexico

Billy the Kid was probably born with the name Henry McCarty. When he was a teenager, his family moved to New Mexico. Before long, he became a thief. He grew up to become one of the most famous outlaws in the Old West. He may have killed more than twenty men. He was gunned down when he was only a young man. His body was buried in Fort Sumner. Now, this village is home to the Billy the Kid Museum.

The caves at Carlsbad Caverns National Park are amazing! If you visit the park, you can go deep underground to see strange rock formations like these.

Santa Fe is known for its museums. One of them is the Museum of Indian Art and Culture. It has beautiful Native jewelry, baskets, and clay pots. Another museum in Santa Fe is El Rancho de las Golondrinas. It focuses on the Spanish settlers. This is a living history museum. Actors dress and speak in the old ways. They show how people lived long ago.

Sports

Sports fans cheer for two minor league teams. The

Scorpions are the state's hockey team. The Isotopes play baseball. Both teams are based in Albuquerque. Many people cheer for the University of New Mexico's teams. All of UNM's teams are called the Lobos. Both their men's and women's basketball teams are often among the best teams in the country.

New Mexico is a center for hot-air ballooning. Each year in October, the biggest hot-air balloon festival in the world takes place in the city of Albuquerque. For more than one week, huge hot-air balloons fill the skies with bright colors.

The state offers other sports, too. The Taos area is well-known for its big ski slopes. The Rio Grande and other rivers are great places to go rafting. People who like to scuba dive head to Santa Rosa. It is a good spot to dive in fresh water.

A skier rockets down a steep slope not far from Taos. Most of New Mexico's ski resorts are near Taos and Santa Fe.

★ ★

adobe — built with bricks made of clay mixed with straw and dried in the sun

alien — having to do with beings from another world

allies — partners

ceremonies — special ways of celebrating important events

colony — a group of people living in a new land but keeping ties with the place they came from

extinct — no longer living or active

mesas — flat-topped hills with steep sides

plateau — a large flat area of land that is higher than the land around it

population — the number of people who live in a place such as a state

potash — matter found in the ground and used for fertilizer for plants

professional — a person who plays a sport for money

rebelled — fought against the people in charge

refinery — a building where oil is processed

reservations — lands set aside by the government for a specific purpose

ruins — the remains of old buildings

territory — land that belongs to a country

UFO — an object in the sky that people do not recognize

wildfire — a fire that burns out of control, usually in the countryside

Books

Celebrating the Powwow. Crabapples (series). Bobbie Kalman (Crabtree)

Colors of the Navajo. Colors of the World (series). Emily Abbink (Carolrhoda Books)

E Is for Enchantment: A New Mexico Alphabet. Discover America State by State (series). Helen Foster James (Sleeping Bear Press)

New Mexico. This Land Is Your Land (series). Ann Heinrichs (Compass Point Books)

The Rio Grande. Rivers of North America (series). Kathleen Fahey (Gareth Stevens)

Web Sites

Enchanted Learning
www.enchantedlearning.com/usa/states/newmexico

Chaco Culture National Historical Park
www.cr.nps.gov/museum/exhibits/chcu

National Atomic Museum: ZOOMzone
www.atomicmuseum.com/tour/zoom.cfm

New Mexico Kids Corner
www.governor.state.nm.us/kidscorner.php

INDEX